# money in your twenties

## Getting Started

Kristen Jacks

Cover design:  Adrienne Luther

ISBN: 978-0-578-61058-0

Dedicated to Bob Jacks

Special thanks to:
Kris Tonski
Donna Fasano
Gerald Whittaker

# Disclaimer

This book is for educational and informational purposes, only. It is not intended to provide financial, legal, tax or investment advice.

Information offered in this book is provided "as is" without any express or implied warranty of any kind, including warranties of fitness for a particular purpose. In no event shall the author, Kristen Jacks, and/or DK Advisors, LLC (d/b/a Money in Your Twenties™) be liable to any party for any damages of any kind, including but not limited to direct, indirect, special or consequential damages for any use of this book including, without limitation, lost profits, tax liability or loss of income.

If you need financial, legal, tax or investment advice, before you make any financial decisions, the author urges you to consult a qualified financial advisor, insurance agent, tax attorney, enrolled agent or other qualified professional who is fully aware of your individual circumstances. The author does not warrant or guarantee the correctness, completeness, accuracy, timeliness or fitness of any information or products or services mentioned in this book.

# Contents

# Introduction

Of all the misconceptions about money, the most unhelpful is the idea that handling money is "common sense." The truth is the opposite. Success with money requires learning things that make no sense (our tax code); learning things that make some sense but require guidance (how to live within your means), and learning things that are totally new like the unique language of money ("premiums," "deductibles," "tax credits").

This book is for young people who aim to make sense of money. This book is also for parents who need more than a vague recollection of the challenges young people face as they begin their money journey.

What are these challenges? The first is one most personal finance books ignore: understanding the significant impact of taxes on income.

Most young people just starting out are unfamiliar with the numerous taxes withheld in paychecks and often surprised by their combined bite. In other words, if your job offer is $60,000, do not spend as though the entire $60,000 awaits.

A single person in my home state of Connecticut who has no "dependents" (you'll find out later why marital status, location, and having kids matter) can expect a tax bill of $13,408 on income of $60,000. Tax liability is even higher in cities like New York and San Francisco which are dream destinations for many young people.

For twentysomethings working in the "gig" economy, tax education is particularly important. Gig workers forego traditional employment where an employer calculates and pays all taxes before paying the worker. Too many gig workers also forego responsible tax payment. They face penalties and interest charges and the headache of owing back taxes.

Beyond taxes, the next big challenge is to live within your means. While student loan debt and high housing costs are obstacles, this book will not tell you to create a budget. Research from the Gallup organization shows that two-thirds of Americans avoid budgets. Plus, the tedious task of logging every purchase is not necessary.

Instead of a budget, this book gives you a step by step **process** for living within your means. The term process is highlighted for a reason. Highly successful organizations embrace the concept of process. An effective process transforms an overwhelming job into a systematic, actionable plan.

When Yale University received 50,015 applications for 2,234 slots in their freshman class (the actual numbers from the 2022 admissions year), Yale ran a process to select the best candidates. When the Recording Academy determines who wins a Grammy, the Academy runs a process. They even share the process with music fans (www.grammy.com/grammys/awards/voting-process).

Financial planning is actually a process. The Certified Financial Planner Board describes financial planning as "the process of determining whether and how an individual can meet life goals through proper management of financial resources."

The six step process in this book will help you calculate your real take home pay and teach you how to allocate it. If you use the process, you will know what you can spend on housing and still have a reasonable amount available for discretionary purchases like clothes and concerts and drinks with friends.

If you stick with this book long enough to tackle taxes and learn how to live within your means, then you will be far ahead of your peers (not to mention people older than you). Feel free to take a victory lap. Then return to this book because there is a more to do.

Handling money well requires juggling more than a few interrelated priorities. While you live within your means, you also need to manage your financial reputation, never miss a debt payment, and minimize risk. This book gives you clear, straightforward guidance on all of these priorities.

The final chapter in this book deals with the unique challenge of managing financial success. Few twentysomethings have high incomes and surplus cash. However, if you took mom's advice and majored in the STEM fields or got a job on Wall Street, then make sure you peruse this chapter.

As you progress through this book, you may start to wonder, "Why didn't I learn this in school?" If the facts and advice in this book are unfamiliar, you are not alone. *The 2017 National Report Card on States Efforts to Improve Financial Literacy in High Schools* exposes the uneven distribution of financial literacy education in America.

While Utah got an "A+" for preparing high school seniors for the real world, more than half the states in the U.S. got a "C," "D" or "F". Connecticut, my home state, got an "F." Worse, the largest state in the union – California – got an "F."

If it bothers you that few states fully prepare high school students to handle money well, then it's time to e-mail your representative in Congress. By the way, Washington, D.C. also got an "F."

Regardless of your home state and what you did or did not learn in school, this book is your guide as you embark on your money journey.

Shall we get started?

# CHAPTER 1

# Income and Its Limitations

In a perfect world, newly minted graduates would have a conversation like this one before renting an apartment or buying a car:

Son: "Mom! Guess what?"

Mom: "What?"

Son: "I got a job offer. The salary is $60,000!"

Mom: "Really? That's great!"

Son:    "I know, right. I can't wait to start my new job. With $60,000 a year, I can get my own place and the new car I've always wanted."

Mom:  "Hold on. You can get your own place OR the new car you've always wanted. Not both."

Son:    "What do you mean? It's SIXTY THOUSAND DOLLARS!"

Mom:  "That's NOT a lot of money."

Son:    "What do you mean?!"

For anyone who has worked only part-time or summers, full-time salaries can sound enormous. Even relatively low hourly compensation for full-time work can feel like a windfall. After all, $12.50 per hour is $100 per day.

Few parents have the facts at their fingertips to help explain why a seemingly large salary or hundreds in weekly pay is insufficient to cover a nice lifestyle. Even if parents name a big ticket expense like a car payment, the cost is dismissed. One can almost imagine the son saying, "I know the car payment is $449, but I'll have $60,000!"

Clearly, there is a need to educate young people about the real purchasing power of income. This education begins with a discussion about taxes.

## The Tax Bite

Recent graduates are often surprised by the combined bite of various income taxes. For example, below are the taxes the son will owe as a resident of Connecticut with the tax status, "single," (you'll learn the importance of location and tax status in the next chapter).

| | |
|---|---|
| $ 60,000 | *Gross* Income |
| $(3,720) | Social Security tax |
| $(870) | Medicare tax |
| $(5,968) | Federal income tax |
| $(<u>2,850</u>) | State income tax |
| | |
| $(13,408) | Total tax liability |
| | |
| $46,592 | *Net* income |

As you can see, the real purchasing power of $60,000 is only $46,592. Taxes take 22% of the $60,000 income.

Does this mean income taxes are always 22%? No. If the son resided in Texas or in Florida, he would pay less because neither state levies an income tax. If he lived in New York City, his tax bill would include a local tax. If he remained in Connecticut and only earned $30,000, he would pay 16%.

Confused? Welcome to the inconsistent patchwork of laws that govern tax liability. The next two chapters cover the basics of income taxes. Get a handle on them before taxes mishandle you.

CHAPTER 2

# Taxes 101

If you could use a good laugh, check out Esquire Magazine's "Dubious Achievement Awards." These awards highlight true stories of misguided accomplishment. For example, a girl scout was honored for selling 300 boxes of cookies in just six hours outside a marijuana dispensary.

Financial planners who work with young people have their own version of the Dubious Achievement Awards. Third place goes to high school seniors who can name every superhero in the *Avengers* movies but not one of the five taxes that come out of a typical paycheck. Second place belongs to college students who know all about Cardi B and nothing about Social Security. First place is for graduates who diligently pay down their student loans then fail to deduct the loan interest on their tax returns.

The goal of this chapter is to give young people the information they need to become as familiar with income taxes as they are with Marvel movies or *Grand Theft Auto* or *The Walking Dead*. Familiarity will help recent graduates anticipate taxes rather than get blindsided by them. Learning the basics will also help young people identify legal ways to pay less tax.

**This chapter covers the essential tax facts that every young adult should know, including:**

- The five taxes that are withheld from paychecks
- Where you live matters
- The W-4
- Tax rates and our "progressive" system
- Deductions and tax credits
- Your magic number

## Taxes that are withheld from paychecks

In a popular meme, Rachel, from the long-running TV show, *Friends*, looks at her paycheck in dismay and says, "Who is FICA and why does he want my money?!"

FICA stands for Federal Insurance Contribution Act and includes two of the five taxes that are withheld from wages in a paycheck. FICA helps fund both Social Security and Medicare programs.

### Social Security

According to the Social Security Administration (SSA), Social Security was created "to promote the economic security of the nation's people." It is "designed to pay retired workers age 65 and older a continuing income after retirement."

The Social Security system is huge. Currently, 169 million Americans pay Social Security taxes and 61 million collect monthly benefits.

Social Security is a fixed-rate tax. **Employees in every state pay 6.2% of their income from work to cover Social Security.**

Most twentysomethings see Social Security only as a big deduction from their paychecks. However, the stated goal of Social Security is to guarantee participants "a continuing income after retirement." In other words, **you already have a retirement account.**

Don't believe me? Visit the Social Security website to create your account. If you have been paying in to the system, then you will see all the amounts you have paid and an estimate of your future benefits. Visit www.ssa.gov to learn more.

## Medicare

Medicare is the federal health insurance program for people who are age 65 or older. It also covers certain younger people with disabilities and people with End-Stage Renal Disease (ESRD).

Like Social Security, Medicare tax is charged at a fixed rate. **Employees in every state pay 1.45% of their income from work to cover Medicare.**

## What's in a name?

As stated above, FICA stands for Federal Insurance Contribution Act and helps to fund both Social Security and Medicare programs. Some paychecks will only show a FICA deduction and some will show separate deductions for Social Security and Medicare.

## The employer match

Employers match the amounts their employees pay for Social Security and Medicare. You pay 7.65% per dollar earned (6.2% for social security and 1.45% for Medicare), and your employer pays 7.65%. The total tax per dollar earned is 15.3%.

Why mention the employer match? Because **self-employed people are on the hook for the entire 15.3%**. This fact is critical for anyone working in the "gig" economy. Failure to set aside adequate funds to pay the 15.3% can lead to serious financial consequences (see "Gig Economy 911").

### The remaining three taxes

Social Security and Medicare (a.k.a. FICA) are just two of the five taxes withheld from paychecks. The other three are federal, state, and local income taxes. Two of these taxes *depend on where you live.*

### Where you live matters

Location! Location! Location! In the United States, you pay zero state income tax if you live in Texas, Florida, Washington, Nevada, South Dakota, Wyoming or Alaska. The remaining 43 states have an income tax, but rates vary. Pennsylvania, Indiana, and North Dakota charge under 4%, while California has the highest marginal tax rate in the country at 13.3%.

Less common but worth mentioning are **local income taxes**. Some cities, counties, and municipalities levy income taxes. In fact, 23 million Americans are hit with local taxes on top of everything else.

### Filling out a W-4

Is your employer nosy? When you start a new job, why does the W-4 worksheet ask your marital status and whether or not your spouse works? And is it your employer's business if you are unmarried and raising a child?

**The W4 form is used by your employer to calculate the correct amount of tax to withhold from your pay.** The W-4 worksheet refers to your marital status and spouse because your federal income tax liability changes depending on your "status." Status is a way the IRS categorizes you in order to give you either a greater tax break or a greater tax burden.

For example, your filing status determines the amount of your **standard deduction.** The standard deduction lowers your federal taxable income. Below are the 2022 standard deduction amounts for the three status options most relevant to twentysomethings.

### 2022 standard deductions by filing status
Single - $12,950
Head of Household - $19,400
Married Filing Jointly - $25,900

Notice that "Head of Household" (HOH) status offers a higher standard deduction than the status "single" even though one must be single to qualify for HOH status.

HOH status applies to single individuals who pay more than half the expenses of caring for a dependent. People with HOH status get tax breaks.

Married people with children can also get tax breaks if their total income from all sources is below a certain threshold.

Due to the complexity of the tax code, the W-4 form does not cover all of the factors that increase or decrease tax liability.

However, it does prompt employees to disclose key, tax-sensitive information.

## Tax rates and our "progressive" tax system

In elementary school, kids learn their times tables. If high school students learned their tax tables, they would anticipate their federal tax bill rather than get blindsided by it.

2022 table of federal tax rates for filing status "single:"

$0 to $10,275 – 10%
$10,275 to $41,775 – 12%
$41,776 to $89,075 – 22%
$89,076 to $170,050 – 24%
$170,051 to $215,950 – 32%
$215,951 to $539,900 – 35%
$539,900 or more – 37%

These tax rates are often referred to as "brackets." Here's how they work. Taxable income is divided among these ranges. The federal government wants 10% of your taxable income below $10,275. It will take 12% of the taxable income that falls between $10,276 and $41,775. Once your taxable income rises above $41,775, you owe 22% of every dollar earned to the federal government. That rises to 24% when taxable income hits $89,076. You get the idea.

For example, recall the young man from the previous chapter who was elated over his job offer of $60,000. His total tax liability is:

| | |
|---|---|
| $ 60,000 | *Gross* Income |
| $(3,720) | Social Security tax |
| $(870) | Medicare tax |
| $(5,968) | Federal income tax |
| $(2,850) | State income tax (CT in this example) |
| $(13,408) | Total tax liability |
| $46,592 | *Net* income |

In this example, Social Security and Medicare taxes are easy to calculate because they are fixed rates (6.2% and 1.45%, respectively). The federal tax is calculated by applying the standard deduction and then using the applicable brackets.

## Calculating federal tax

### Step 1: Apply standard deduction

| | |
|---|---|
| $60,000 | Gross income |
| $(12,950) | Standard deduction for status "single" |
| $47,050 | "adjusted" gross income |

### Step 2: Apply brackets for status "single"

The first $10,275 is taxed at 10%

$10,275 x 10% = $1,027

The dollars between $10,276 and $41,775 are taxed at 12%.

($41,775 - $10,276) x .12 = $31,499 x .12 = $3,780

The remaining adjusted gross income is taxed at 22%.

Find this remaining amount by taking the adjusted gross income from above (i.e., the salary minus the standard deduction) and subtracting the income we have already taxed (yes – this is confusing!).

Remaining income = $47,050 - $10,275 - $31,499 = $5,276

Apply the 22% tax rate to the remaining income:

$5,276 x .22 = $1,161

Add all three tax amounts to get the total Federal tax:

$1,027 + $3,780 + $1,161 = $5,968

Yay! You did it!

Like the standard deduction, tax brackets depend on filing status. **Notice that the brackets for "Head of Household" (HOH) are more favorable than the brackets for "single"** for taxable income below $55,900.

2022 table of federal tax rates for Head of Household
$0 to $14,650 – 10%
$14,651 to $55,900 – 12%
$55,901 to $89,050 – 22%

Regardless of status, all Federal income taxes are *progressive.* The *percentage* owed increases as income rises.

## Deductions and tax credits

In the prior sections, you learned that FICA taxes are fixed rates while federal, state, and local taxes vary. Deductions and credits add another layer of complexity to our tax system.

**Deductions reduce the amount of income that is subject to tax. Credits directly reduce the amount of tax owed**.

Identifying deductions and credits to which you may be entitled is a much better use of your time than binge-watching Netflix. You can legally lower your tax bill if you endeavor to learn this area of the tax code.

Yes, you have to do it yourself. There is no friendly, neighborhood IRS office in each town staffed with people whose job it is to help taxpayers find legal ways to pay less tax. Instead, the IRS offers you its website (www.irs.gov), and tons of helpful videos on YouTube.

At the time of this writing, "Credits and Deductions" is a highly visible button on the IRS homepage. And, for certain credits and deductions, the IRS provides an Interactive Tax Assistant (ITA) to help you determine if you qualify.

It's a quirky system, but the myriad deductions and credits to which you *may* be entitled make filing your taxes somewhat like **the ultimate open book test**.

If do-it-yourself is not your thing, then you can rely on tax software and hope it prompts you with the right questions to identify deductions and credits. However, this option is a bit like using GPS when you have no idea where you are going. A minor input mistake might lead you off-track.

You can also hire a tax professional. How to do that is covered in the final chapter of this book, "Managing Success."

One last note on deductions. You may have heard you cannot use any other deductions if you take the standard deduction. Not true.

If you take the standard deduction, then you cannot also deduct certain expenses that are specifically grouped as itemized deductions. These include donations to charities, payments for state and local taxes, and mortgage interest.

However, you may be entitled to "adjustments to income" which are grouped with deductions on the IRS website. For example, you may be able to lower your taxable income by deducting the interest you paid on student loans if you meet certain criteria.

In his book, *The Seven Habits of Highly Effective People,* Stephen R. Covey argues that successful people begin with the end in mind. Tax-wise, the "end" is filing your taxes. To do this, you fill out and submit Form 1040 and its applicable schedules.

To succeed with credits and deductions, take a look online at the Form 1040 and its schedules. You'll see the many ways taxpayers are invited to use deductions and credits if they qualify.

If you feel overwhelmed by the process of finding credits and deductions, then definitely consult a tax professional. See "How to Select a Tax Professional" in the final chapter of this book, "Managing Success."

### A few words about income
This chapter covers the tax consequences of income from work. Few twentysomethings have significant income from other sources like rental income or stock dividends.

The IRS taxes most forms of income. You will owe more in taxes than what is calculated here if you have additional income outside of work. You are advised to consult a tax professional.

## Your magic number

As previously noted, federal income taxes are *progressive.* The *percentage* owed increases as income rises.

Few twentysomethings fret over the progressive nature of our tax system because their income falls in the 10% or 12% bracket. However, all young adults should know that the bracket after 12% is 22%.

People who are good with money are keenly aware of the point at which their income crosses into the 22% bracket. At Money in Your Twenties℠, we call this point your "magic number."

Not everyone has the same magic number because it depends on your tax status. To learn how to calculate your magic number, visit the final chapter of this book, "Managing Success."

# CHAPTER 3

# Taxes and the Gig Economy

Imagine you visit an unusual town. Drivers in this town are careful to avoid each other, but they do not stop for red lights. In fact, the street lights have no effect at all on the flow of traffic. Somehow, everyone gets where they are going without following the rules.

For twentysomethings, the gig economy is like this town. Young people enjoy co-working spaces humming with activity; they do graphic design or teach yoga or play guitar. They rely on apps to find opportunities to drive people to the airport or run errands or deliver packages. And, they don't follow the rules. What rules? Tax rules.

Recall from the last chapter the five taxes that come out of a typical paycheck: Social Security, Medicare, federal, state, and local taxes. If you earn income from gig work, the rules say **you owe these taxes whether an employer withholds them or not.**

Consider drivers for Uber or Lyft. They receive lump sum payments for their work rather than a traditional paycheck. Uber and Lyft drivers are "independent contractors." Independent contractors must calculate the tax they owe and send it to the IRS or face serious financial consequences.

Some young people do not know they are independent contractors. Take the example of Bree, a 22 year old yoga instructor. Bree works part-time for Balance Yoga. She considers herself an employee of the yoga studio because she was "hired" by the owner; she gets her teaching schedule from the owner, and she listens to the owner's feedback.

However, Bree does not receive a paycheck with taxes withheld. The owner of Balance Yoga pays Bree a lump sum and considers her an "independent contractor," not an employee.

Bree thinks independent contractors work on houses and hang sheet rock. She has no idea she is supposed to set aside money for taxes and pay them on a regular basis. Poor Bree. She could owe a lot of money in back taxes, interest, and penalties if she doesn't figure out her situation soon.

## Big problem

How relevant is this problem for young people? According to the Federal Reserve's *2018 Survey of Household Economics and Decision-making* (SHED), **33% of adults under age thirty say they earn money through gig work or self-employment.** Yet, many of these novice taxpayers are unfamiliar with tax rules.

H&R Block, the tax preparation giant, agrees. On its website, H&R Block says the #1 problem for the newly self-employed is tax ignorance which "can result in a large tax bill you didn't know about."

The IRS isn't helping the situation by using outdated examples to describe self-employment. If you visit the IRS website (www.irs.gov) and search "independent contractor," this explanation appears:

"People such as doctors, dentists, veterinarians, lawyers, accountants, contractors, subcontractors, public stenographers, or auctioneers who are in an independent trade, business, or profession in which they offer their services to the general public are generally independent contractors."

This definition is not relatable to people under thirty. Doctors, dentists, vets, and lawyers all have advanced degrees and perform highly specialized services. What does their work have to do with driving someone to the airport?

## Self-employment tax

What's the biggest disconnect between young gig workers and tax reality? Self-employment tax. Self-employment tax is mostly Social Security.

Think of anything that is huge in your world and virtually unknown in the world of much older people. Examples like Thanos, WhatsApp, and Millie Bobby Brown come to mind.

Now, reverse this. What is absolutely critical to older Americans and barely recognizable to you? Social Security. Sixty-one million people collect social security, and, for one in three people over the age of 65, Social Security is their only source of income.

Recall from the previous chapter that FICA taxes (Social Security and Medicare) are fixed rates. Employees in every state pay 6.2% of their income to cover Social Security and 1.45% for Medicare. **Employers match these percentages for a total of 15.3% of every dollar earned.**

Even if twentysomethings are familiar with FICA, most do not know that employers pay an equal portion of Social Security and Medicare taxes on behalf of their workers. If twentysomethings understood the role of the employer, then they would be less surprised by the taxes they owe when they work in the "gig" economy.

In the gig economy, the traditional employer is absent. The worker is responsible for *double* the amount of Social Security and

Medicare because he or she has to pay both portions.

For the gig worker, the 15.3% that covers the employee and employer contributions to Social Security and Medicare is essentially renamed "self-employment tax" and the gig worker is on the hook for the entire amount.

### Pay-as-you-go

H&R Block says tax ignorance is the #1 problem for the newly self-employed. The #2 problem is "I didn't know I had to pay throughout the year."

Here is a helpful explanation from the IRS website:

"Taxes are pay-as-you-go, and making estimated tax payments is HOW you pay-as-you-go. Taxpayers use estimated tax payments to pay both income tax and self-employment tax (Social Security and Medicare). If you don't pay enough tax, through either withholding or estimated tax, or a combination of both, you may have to pay a penalty.

The payment of estimated tax for the first quarter of the calendar year (that is, January through March) is due on April 15. Payments for subsequent quarters are due on June 15, September 15 and January 15. If you don't pay enough by these dates you may be charged a penalty even if you're due a refund when you file your tax return."

### The parental disconnect

You might be thinking, if all of this confusing and costly stuff is true, why didn't my parents tell me? Welcome to a generation gap on steroids.

The gig economy is new, but the side hustle is timeless. When your parents were young, they could raise extra cash by babysitting or mowing lawns or painting houses. These arrangements were between individuals, not between an individual and a business.

Businesses are obligated to report to the IRS any payments to individuals that exceed $600 in a calendar year. They comply by sending a 1099-MISC form to the gig worker and a copy of the 1099-MISC form to the IRS.

While the law technically requires individuals to report income paid to household workers, the threshold amount is over $2,000, and some individuals fail to report income over the threshold (google "nanny gate" for details).

In other words, today's side hustle initiates an electronic paper trail for the IRS. Don't blame your parents if they didn't warn you. Their side hustle was paperless.

### The fix

Does this chapter describe your situation? Don't panic. You don't actually owe 15.3% of self-employment tax on every dollar you received from gig work.

Independent contractors are allowed to deduct reasonable business expenses from the income they receive for work. In fact, self-employed people must determine a "net income" number that is subject to self-employment tax and federal income tax. State and local taxes may also apply depending on where you live and the amount of your net income.

Go to the IRS website and check out Publication 535 ("Business Expenses"). Pub. 535 discusses common business expenses and explains what is and what is not deductible.

If you are overwhelmed by the idea of making your own quarterly tax payments, you have a solution. **If you mix gig work with a regular job, then your traditional employer can increase your withholdings to cover your estimated taxes from gig work.**

### What about federal, state and local taxes?

Yes, gig workers are subject to federal tax, and to state and local taxes if they apply. However, **gig workers can deduct one-half of the self-employment tax on their federal returns.**

Still confused? You are not alone. Self-employment increases the difficulty of tax compliance, and new rules ushered in by the Tax Cuts and Jobs Act (like the "qualified business income deduction") are not straightforward.

That's why hiring a tax professional may be the best business investment you make all year. To find out how to select a tax professional, see the final chapter of this book, "Managing Success."

CHAPTER **4**

# The Process℠
## Six Steps for Living within Your Means

In the chapter, "Income and Its Limitations," we meet an exuberant young man who believes that his $60,000 job offer will cover the cost of a new car and an apartment without a roommate. He is surprised when his mom says he can't afford both.

While some twentysomethings will curtail their spending plans based solely on parental advice, wouldn't it be helpful if all young adults could figure out for themselves what they can afford?

Well, they can. Money in Your Twenties℠ presents **The Process**℠.

The Process℠ enables you to **predict** what you can afford based on only a few inputs. The Process℠ calculates an accurate amount to spend on rent and other recurring expenses and includes an allowance for discretionary spending. Most importantly, The Process℠ helps you clarify what you most want and helps you get what you want without overspending.

The Process℠ works whether you earn a modest hourly wage or $75,000 per year. It works if you want to live in an expensive city while carrying mountains of debt. It even works if you are a shopaholic.

Best of all, The Process℠ is simple. Anyone who can subtract, divide, and prioritize can succeed with The Process℠.

### The Process™ is not a budget

Trying to understand what you can afford by listing every possible expense is a good way to feel overwhelmed and a poor way to live within your means. That's why this book will not tell you to create a budget.

Instead of a budget, you need a process. Highly successful organizations embrace the concept of process. A solid process transforms an overwhelming task into a clear, actionable plan.

If your aim is to succeed with money, you need a process to determine what you can afford and what you really want. You need

The Process<sup>SM</sup>.

The Process<sup>SM</sup> is simply these six steps:

Step 1 – Estimate your annual income
Step 2 – Deduct taxes to find net income
Step 3 – Think monthly (divide net income by 12)
Step 4 – Divide monthly net income by three to evenly fund three allowances: rent, other recurring expenses, and discretionary spending
Step 5 – Get clear about recurring expenses
Step 6 – Shift money within the three allowances to create a spending plan that suits your needs and priorities.

## Using The Process<sup>SM</sup>

The Process moves money conversations from the subjective (feelings and wishful thinking) to the objective (actual numbers). With the help of The Process<sup>SM</sup>, the mom and son from Chapter One do not have to argue. They simply have to follow the six steps to determine what the son can afford.

Let's use their situation to demonstrate how The Process<sup>SM</sup> works.

## Step 1 – Estimate your annual income

Answer: $60,000 (the son's salary from his job offer)

## Step 2 – Deduct taxes to find net income

Taxes are $13,408 (see Chapter One)

Net income:  $60,000 - $13,408 = $46,592

Review the chapter, "Taxes 101." All earners pay 6.2% for Social Security and 1.45% for Medicare. The remaining taxes vary depending on your tax status, location, and income.

While taxes are daunting, they are also predictable. Understanding taxes is critical to managing money well.

## Step 3 – Think monthly (divide net income by 12)

Answer:  $46,592/12 = $3,882.66

Thinking monthly is new if you currently enjoy the dual buffer zone of school (one bill per semester) and parents (who often cover monthly bills like phone or car payment).

Learn to think monthly because most recurring bills are monthly.

## Step 4 – Divide monthly net income by three to evenly fund three allowances: rent, other recurring expenses, and discretionary spending

Answer: $3,882.66/3 = $1,294.22

Step 4 creates a framework for all future spending. This step divides net income into three equal amounts: an **accurate rent allowance**, adequate funds for other recurring bills (e.g., groceries, student loan payment, phone plan), and ample money for discretionary spending (think clothes, dining out, paying down debt, and saving).

The beauty of Step 4 is its simplicity. All you have to do is take your monthly net income and divide by three (geek alert – to learn why the process works mathematically, see the end of this chapter).

The son now has these three allowances:

Spending Allowances:
Rent: $1,294.22
Other recurring expenses: $1,294.22
Discretionary: $1,294.22

## Step 5 – Get clear about recurring expenses

It is easy to underestimate recurring expenses. That's why Money in Your Twenties™ lists the 24 most common ones on its website. Visit www.moneyinyourtwenties.com and click the button "Know Your Nut" (nut is an informal term for recurring expenses).

The son visits the website and views the recurring expenses listed in the Know Your Nut section.  He clicks the ones that will apply if he gets a new car and his own place.

He **does not include rent**.   These are his "other" recurring expenses.

He hits "next" to view his customized list.

## Recurring expenses:
Groceries
Car loan/lease
Student Loan
Car insurance
Gas for Car
Electricity
Internet/WiFi
Gas
Phone Plan
Laundry/DC
Personal Care
Subs (streaming)
Gym Membership

Now the son enters amounts for each expense. The website tallies his entries.

Some costs he knows exactly (his student loan payment and phone plan); some costs require him to ask friends and family for estimates; some costs he finds on the internet (e.g., monthly car loan payment calculator).

**<u>Recurring Expenses with Costs:</u>**

| | |
|---|---|
| Groceries | $250 |
| Car loan/lease | $449 |
| Student Loan | $220 |
| Car insurance | $246 |
| Gas for Car | $100 |
| Electricity | $70 |
| Internet/WiFi | $60 |
| Gas | $20 |
| Phone Plan | $80 |
| Laundry/DC | $10 |
| Personal Care | $20 |
| Subs (streaming) | $20 |
| Gym Membership | $30 |
| | |
| Total: | $1,575.00 |

Yikes! Clearly $1,575.00 exceeds the son's "other recurring expenses" allowance of $1,294.22

The true cost of a new car and living on one's own is surprising to the son. Meanwhile, his mom is relieved that The Process<sup>SM</sup>

moved a sensitive conversation about money from the subjective to the objective.

Now the mom and son use Step 6 to see if shifting money within the three allowances can rescue the son's plan.

### Step 6 – Shift money within the three allowances to create a spending plan that suits your needs and priorities.

Step 6 is all about the "personal" in "personal finance." In Step 6, you take the three allowances and shift money where you want it most.

Do you long to live in a cool city like New York or San Francisco? Step 6 allows you to boost your rent allocation by shifting money from either recurring expenses or discretionary funds or both.

Are you a debt-buster/saver? In Step 6, you can increase your discretionary allowance in order to pay down debt and boost savings.

Do you like to strike a balance? Then keep rent, other recurring bills, and discretionary spending equal.

**Regardless of your personal preferences, you only need to follow one rule: the three allowances combined must not exceed your monthly net income.**

Circling back to the son, we find him grappling with the reality that his recurring bills will be staggering if he lives on his own and buys a new car.

Using Step 6, he begins to weigh his options. Instead of the standard, equal allocation of money to the three allowances, he considers shifting money from discretionary spending to boost recurring expenses.

Recall he needs $1,575.00 to cover recurring bills. He shifts $280.78 from his discretionary allowance to his other recurring expenses allowance.

His new spending plan looks like this:

*Adjusted* Allowances:
Rent: $1,294.22
Other recurring expenses: $1,575.00
Discretionary: $1,013.44

Total: $3,882.66      (Make sure total matches net income)

Now, the son thinks about this plan. Each month he must spend $2,869.22 (rent plus other recurring expenses). Only $1,013.44 remains for vacations, dining out, shopping, paying down debt, and saving.

He wonders, "Isn't it irresponsible to make $60,000 per year without a clear plan to pay down debt and to save?"

### Adding a roommate

You don't need to read Harvard's *State of the Nation's Housing* study to know that rents have skyrocketed in the past several decades. The fact is that life without a roommate is financially unattainable for most recent graduates.

This sobering fact is sinking in for the son. He decides to use Step 6 to see what adding a roommate will accomplish. First, he changes his rent allowance to $1,000 because he knows he can get a nice two bedroom in his area for $2,000/month.

The son also lowers some of his recurring expenses since a roommate will pay half of the utilities.

| Recurring Expenses: | | With a roommate |
|---|---|---|
| Groceries | $250 | $250 |
| Car loan/lease | $449 | $449 |
| Student Loan | $220 | $220 |
| Car insurance | $246 | $246 |
| Gas for Car | $100 | $100 |
| **Electricity** | **$70** | **$35** |
| **Internet/WiFi** | **$60** | **$30** |
| **Gas** | **$20** | **$10** |
| Phone Plan | $80 | $80 |

| | | |
|---|---|---|
| Laundry | $10 | $10 |
| Personal Care | $20 | $20 |
| Subs (streaming) | $20 | $20 |
| Gym Membership | $30 | $30 |
| | | |
| Total: | $1,575.00 | $1,500.00 |

In his allowances, the son shifts rent savings ($294.22) and recurring expense savings ($75) to discretionary income. His adjusted allowances now look like this:

**Adjusted Allowances:**
Rent: $1,000.00
Other recurring expenses: $1,500.00
Discretionary: $1,382.66

Total: $3,882.66

Success! The son is happy with this plan. He can move out, buy a new car, and still have money each month for paying down debt, saving, buying cool stuff, and spontaneous fun.

### The Process™ for hourly workers

The Process works for hourly employees even if they earn a modest wage.  For example, Maria is paid $12.50 per hour at a retail job. She uses The Process™ to see if she can afford to live on her own.

### Step 1 – Estimate your annual income

Here's a tip for full-time hourly workers. Estimate your annual income by multiplying your hourly wage by 2,000. This works if you plan to work 40 hours per week for 50 weeks (40 x 50 = 2,000).

In Maria's case, her annual income estimate is:

$12.50 x 2,000 hours = $25,000.00

### Step 2 – Deduct taxes to find net income

Income from work is always subject to three taxes: Social Security, Medicare, and federal tax. Lucky for Maria, she lives in Texas and pays no state tax. Her town has no local tax.

Maria's tax liability looks like this:

| $1,550 | Social Security tax – 6.2% |
|---|---|
| $ 363 | Medicare tax – 1.45% |
| $1,342 | Federal income tax |
| $3,255 | Total tax liability |

Net income:

$25,000 - $3,255 = $21,745 net income

## Step 3 – Think monthly (divide net income by 12)

Net income of $21,745 divided by 12 is $1,812.08

## Step 4 – Divide monthly net income by three to evenly fund three allowances: rent, other recurring expenses, and discretionary spending

$1,812.08 divided by three is $604.03. Here are Maria's spending allowances:

Spending Allowances:
Rent: $604.03
Other recurring expenses: $604.03
Discretionary: $604.03
Total: $1,812.09

### Step 5 – Get clear about recurring expenses

Maria's parents bought her a used car in high school. She has no car payment but does pay for car insurance and gas.

Maria visits the Money in Your Twenties℠ website to review recurring expenses. She clicks on the expenses she will have if she shares an apartment with two roommates.

She **does *not* include rent**. These are her "other" recurring expenses.

She enters actual and estimated costs.

Recurring expenses:

| | | |
|---|---|---|
| Groceries | $250 | |
| Car insurance | $180 | |
| Gas for Car | $80 | |
| Electric | $40 | (Utilities shared with |
| Gas | $10 | two roommates) |
| Internet/Wifi | $40 | |
| Phone Plan | $80 | |
| Subs (streaming) | $20 | |
| Laundry/DC | $40 | |
| Personal Care | $50 | |
| Gym Membership | $35 | |
| | | |
| Total: | $825.00 | |

**Step 6 – Shift money within the three allowances to create a spending plan that suits your needs and priorities.**

In order to move out and live with roommates, Maria will have to lower her discretionary spending and/or rent allowances to cover her recurring bills.

Maria believes she can lower her rent to $500.00. If she sifts the savings (604.03 – 500.00 = 104.03) to recurring bills, she has $604.03 + $104.03 = $708.06. This number falls $116.94 short of the necessary $825.00.

Maria reviews her list of recurring bills. There's nothing she is willing to cut. Maria will have to lower discretionary spending to $487.09 to cover recurring expenses ($604.03 - $116.94). Her adjusted allowances look like this:

<u>Adjusted Allowances</u>:
Rent: $500.00
Other recurring expenses: $825.00
Discretionary: $487.09

Total: $1,812.09

Maria is discouraged. She loves to eat out with friends and buy new clothes. How will she live on only $487.09 of discretionary spending each month?

Maria decides to delay moving out until she takes on a side job. She loves dogs and plans to offer her services for pet care. She may also look into Apps that pair available workers with quick work assignments.

### The Process™ for expensive cities

Expensive cities like New York are dream destinations for some young adults. Here's a look at how far $50,000 per year stretches in NYC.

**Step 1 – Estimate your annual income**
      Answer: $50,000

**Step 2 – Deduct taxes to find net income**

People in New York City pay five income taxes: Social Security, Medicare, federal, state, and local taxes. This example assumes the earner has the tax status "single."

Taxes for income of $50,000

| | |
|---|---|
| $3,100 | Social Security tax |
| $ 725 | Medicare tax |
| $4,342 | Federal income tax |
| $2,348 | New York State tax |
| $1,508 | New York City tax |
| | |
| $12,023 | Total tax liability |

Net income calculation:

$50,000 - $12,023 = $37,977

## Step 3 – Think monthly (divide net income by 12)

$37,977 divided by 12 is $3,164.75

## Step 4 – Divide monthly net income by three to evenly fund three allowances: rent, other recurring expenses, and discretionary spending

$3,164.75 divided by 3 is $1,054.92.

<u>Spending Allowances</u>:
Rent: $1,054.92
Other recurring expenses: $1,054.92
Discretionary: $1,054.92

Total: $3,164.76

## Step 5 – Get clear about recurring expenses

In NYC, people save money by using mass transit instead of a car, but they pay more for everything from groceries to a gym membership.

Here is a sample of typical recurring expenses for a single adult with one roommate. Remember, rent is excluded. These are the "other recurring expenses."

### Recurring expenses for single adult with one roommate:

| | |
|---|---|
| Groceries | $350 |
| Student loans: | $250 |
| Subway/Bus Fare | $127  (unlimited monthly MetroCard) |
| Electricity | $70 |
| Internet/WiFi | $60 |
| Gas | $20 |
| Phone Plan | $80 |
| Laundry/DC | $50 |
| Personal Care | $50 |
| Subs (streaming) | $20 |
| Gym Membership | $70 |
| | |
| Total: | $1,147.00 |

### Step 6 – Shift money within the three allowances to create a spending plan that suits your needs and priorities.

When it comes to the cost of rent in NYC, it's hard to distinguish urban legend from fact. One reputable website claims the *average* rent for a two-bedroom apartment in Manhattan is $3,662.00. This number includes luxury high rises.

If we go with a cheap walk-up in a safe neighborhood, then the *median* rent of $2,600.00 is appropriate. Each roommate pays $1,300.00.

In this example, the allowances for rent and recurring expenses are increased and discretionary spending is decreased in order to reach monthly net income of $3,164.75.

*Adjusted* Allowances:
Rent:  $1,300.00
Other recurring expenses: $1,147.00
Discretionary: $717.75

Total:  $3,164.75

## Does The Process™ work with higher incomes?
Yes. However, The Process℠ does not account for 401(k) or IRA contributions which become crucial once you start to earn enough to place you in the 22% federal tax bracket.

For example, note the tax burden on someone with the tax status "single" who lives in CT and earns $75,000 per year:

| | |
|---|---|
| $4,650 | Social Security tax |
| $1,088 | Medicare tax |
| $9,675 | Federal income tax |
| $3,756 | CT State tax |
| | |
| $19,169 | Total tax liability |

Clearly, this individual should use a tax-advantaged retirement account to lower taxable income.

Here are the spending allowances if **no tax shelter** is used.

### Step 1 – Estimate your annual income
Answer: $75,000

### Step 2 – Deduct taxes to find net income
Net income calculation:

$75,000 - $19,169 = $55,831

### Step 3 – Think monthly (divide net income by 12)

$55,831 divided by 12 is $4,652.58

### Step 4 – Divide monthly net income by three to evenly fund three allowances: rent, other recurring expenses, and discretionary spending

$4,652.58 divided by 3 is $1,550.86

Spending Allowances:
Rent: $1,550.86
Other recurring expenses: $1,550.86
Discretionary: $1,550.86

Total: $4,652.58

In the case of income that hits the 22% federal tax bracket or a higher bracket, The Process<sup>SM</sup> is useful to identify an initial "ball-park" allowance for rent, other recurring expenses, and discretionary spending. However, the use of tax-advantaged accounts will change the reportable income number and subsequent tax liability.

If your income is relatively high, then see the last chapter of this book, "Managing Success."

## The Process™ and saving

The Process allocates one-third of your take home pay to "discretionary." While many enticing items and experiences compete for your discretionary dollars, you will thank me later if you get in the habit now of paying down debt and saving.

If setting aside money today feels like too much of a sacrifice, then start small and increase your debt reduction/savings every time you get a raise. If you make your savings automatic, then you won't miss the money because you never got used to having it.

To learn which savings vehicles are best and/or which loans to pay down first, read the chapter, "The New Way to Save."

## Geek alert

The Process℠ is the antidote to overspending. It is also sound math.

A widely accepted financial planning rule is to limit rent to 28% of gross income. In The Process℠, rent is exactly 28% of gross income when taxes are 15%. As taxes increase, rent as a percentage of gross income decreases, but only slightly.

# Your Turn
Use The Process℠ for your unique situation

---

## Step 1 – Estimate your annual income

## Step 2 – Deduct taxes to find net income
Remember that Social Security and Medicare are fixed amounts.
The remaining three taxes depend on things like your filing status,
location, income, credits, and deductions.

**Step 3 – Think monthly (divide net income by 12)**


**Step 4 – Divide monthly net income by three to evenly fund three allowances: rent, other recurring expenses, and discretionary spending**

Spending Allowances:
Rent:
Other recurring expenses:
Discretionary:

# Step 5 – Get clear about recurring expenses

Visit moneyinyourtwenties.com to view the most common recurring expenses

## Step 6 – Shift money within the three allowances to create a spending plan that suits your needs and priorities.


Adjusted Allowances:
Rent:
Other recurring expenses:
Discretionary:


NOTES:

# CHAPTER 5

# Know Your Nut

The Process™ enables young adults to predict what they can afford for big ticket items like rent or a car. It is a terrific tool for seniors nearing graduation, recent graduates, and young adults who are ready for their own apartment.

If you have already committed to big expenses like rent, then you may have skipped the last chapter. However, The Process™ can help you live within your means at any time. To see if you need The Process™, find the total amount you spend each month on recurring expenses.

It is far too easy to underestimate recurring bills. That's why Money in Your Twenties™ lists the 24 most common ones on its website. Visit www.moneyinyourtwenties.com and click the button "Know Your Nut" (nut is an informal term for the bills you have to pay each month).

The most common recurring expenses are also listed in this chapter for your convenience.

On the website, select all the expenses that apply to your situation then click "next." The website shows only your list. Now add amounts. The website tallies your entries and gives you a total at the bottom of the screen.

Unlike in The Process℠, you should include rent. Once you have a grand total for recurring expenses including rent, compare it to your monthly take home pay (the amount you get to keep after all taxes have been withheld).

Your recurring expenses should be less than 70% of your take home pay.

If you are spending more than 70% of your take home pay on monthly bills, then you must follow the six steps of The Process℠ to prioritize and to re-balance spending. You cannot succeed with money until you live within your means.

## Common recurring expenses

Rent or mortgage
Groceries
Car loan/lease
Student Loans
Car insurance
Gas for Car
Parking/Tolls
Subway/Bus Fare
Electricity
Internet/WiFi
Gas
Phone Plan
Cable
Subs (streaming)
Water
Garbage
Laundry/DC
Personal Care
Credit Cards
Gym Membership
Health Insurance
Taxes Not Withheld
Child Care
Other

Note: if you build your own list on the Money in Your Twenties℠ website, then you can save it for future use.

CHAPTER 6

# Giving You Credit

If you participated in the college admissions process, then you probably had multiple colleges request your High School transcript and SAT or ACT scores. They used this information to predict your ability to handle college-level work and to compare you to other applicants.

Beyond academics, all sorts of decision-makers want to assess what you can handle and compare you to others. Lenders, and some landlords and employers, evaluate you using **credit reports and credit scores.**

## Credit reports and scores

The notion that the best predictor of future behavior is past behavior underpins the use of credit reports and credit scores.

Lenders, and some landlords and employers, want to see how you handled borrowing in the past to predict if you will be responsible in the future. They rely on credit reports and credit scores to evaluate you.

**A credit report** shows a consumer's borrowing history and use of credit. It includes payment history on loans (e.g., student loans and auto loans), and credit accounts (e.g., credit and store cards). Car lease payments are also tracked on credit reports.

In much the same way that a "D" looks bad on a report card, delinquent accounts on a credit report are a red flag for lenders, landlords, and employers. While decision-makers may overlook a late payment or two, they definitely do not want to see any accounts ending in collection or charge-off.

**Credit scores** are based on information found in credit reports. They are valued by decision-makers as a quick assessment tool. While credit reports can be very data dense, a credit score is one number that gives decision-makers an immediate sense of a consumer's creditworthiness.

The most well-known credit scores are FICO scores. FICO scores generally range from 300 to 850. Scores in the low 700s or above are considered good. Scores over 800 are exceptional.

High achievers take note. One factor in credit scores is length of credit history. For this reason, you may not be able to achieve an exceptional score even if your payment history is impeccable. You simply haven't been borrowing long enough.

## Viewing your credit reports and scores

Equifax, Experian, and TransUnion are the three main data companies that collect information used in credit reports and credit scores. Sometimes referred to as "credit bureaus," these companies operate independently from each other which is why individuals have more than one credit report.

According to the Federal Trade Commission, you are entitled to one **free** copy of your credit report every 12 months from each of these companies. You can order your credit reports online from annualcreditreport.com, the only authorized website for free credit reports, or call 1-877-322-8228.

Make sure you have your **social security number.** You will need it to obtain your reports.

**Credit scores** take a bit more work to obtain for free. Some banks and credit card companies provide credit scores to their customers. There are also popular websites that provide them. However, most of these sites also push credit cards. For that reason, they are not listed here.

### Does everyone have a credit report?

If you have not used credit, then you do not have a credit report. The good news is that you have zero risk of mishandling credit if you don't use it. The bad news is that you cannot demonstrate how trustworthy you are if you do not have a credit report.

If you plan to borrow money in the future (for example, to purchase a car) or if you want to look good to landlords and employers, then you should obtain a form of credit and use it, wisely.

### Looking good

Since you are a responsible borrower, you may be thinking "I got this! My reports and scores will be good." Not so fast. While the system is *supposed* to measure creditworthiness, it has quirks that can make you look bad even when you are being good.

Say you only have one credit card and you carry a very low balance. When you get the bill, you owe less than $40.00. Since this is a small sum and you are a busy person, you decide to skip a payment and pay in full on the next bill. Guess what? Your financial reputation just took a hit. Why? Because **on time bill payment is the single biggest factor** in your credit score.

While paying small amounts on time is a hassle, the good news is that you can attain a solid financial reputation on a tight budget. Remember, the most important factor in your credit score is on time payment – not how much money you have.

**The second biggest factor in your score is your "utilization ratio."** The utilization ratio is a measure of how much available credit you use.

This may sound complicated but think of it this way. How would you feel if your friend had a dozen donuts and ate all of them? That's how lenders feel when you have access to a $1,000 credit limit and charge $999. Yuck.

Self-restraint connotes maturity. Keep credit card balances below 30% of your available credit. If you want to look really good, use only 10% or less.

To learn the five main factors that influence your credit scores, visit the Money in Your Twenties℠ website (www.moneyinyourtwenties.com).

### Rewards of good credit

People with good credit qualify for lower interest rates on loans and credit card balances. The savings from lower interest rates can be substantial.

Good credit can also impress employers and reassure landlords. Whether you want the loan, the apartment or the job, good credit helps you.

### Errors and identity theft

You can do everything right and still not look good to lenders, landlords, and employers. Why? Errors on your credit report can harm your reputation and impact your credit scores. In the worst-case scenario, you may be the victim of identity theft.

Carefully read your credit reports to make sure that the information on each account is accurate. If you find mistakes, immediately contact both the credit bureau and the account provider.

If accounts that you did not open appear on your credit report, then you may be the victim of identity theft. Visit the Federal Trade Commission's site, IdentityTheft.gov, to report the theft and to start a recovery plan. You should also contact one of the three credit bureaus. Confirm with the one you contact that they will handle alerting the other two bureaus.

Finally, reach out to the company that holds the fraudulent account. Alert them and keep a record of your communication with the company.

Depending on the nature of the error or fraud, you may need to change passwords or even change your driver's license number. Each case is different. Make sure you are vigilant and thorough. Your financial reputation depends on it.

CHAPTER 7

# Student Loans and Other Debt

*"Figuring out how much to pay for a college education is one of the biggest financial decisions people make in their lifetime, and parents often leave the final call to a 17-year-old who has never purchased anything more expensive than a bicycle."*

Ron Lieber, the "Your Money" columnist for *The New York Times*

One could argue that society is slow to respond to dangers ushered in by change. Take the automobile. While there were a million cars on the road by 1913, standardized driver's education did not exist until the 1930s, and South Dakota did not require a driver's license until 1954.

Today, there is considerable concern about the proliferation of student loan debt, and plenty of calls for something to be done. Yet, meaningful change is not on the horizon, and borrowing continues, unabated.

This chapter addresses the enormous responsibility of managing student loans and other debt. Read it before you crash financially.

## Pause before you borrow

This book is for twentysomethings, not teens. Most likely, you have already made your borrowing decisions related to college. That's why this chapter focuses on repaying student loans.

However, if you delayed going to college or wonder if you should switch schools to lower your future debt burden, then definitely pause before you borrow (or borrow more).

Ideally, college should be a good value. *Kiplinger's Personal Finance Magazine* considers a school a good value if it delivers a high-quality education at an affordable price.

Affordable does not mean cheap. *Kiplinger's* points out that high quality private schools can be a good value if they have lower than average tuition or generous financial aid or both.

If you haven't enrolled in a college or you are willing to transfer, check out *Kiplinger's* "Best College Values" in the August 2019 issue. The magazine ranks hundreds of colleges and universities. It shows total cost before and after financial aid. Most importantly, *Kiplinger's* publishes the average debt burden of each school's recent graduates.

## Repaying student loans

If you are finished or almost finished with school then it is time to learn how to repay student loans, responsibly.

The first rule for repaying your student loans is, "Be proactive." Investigate your repayment options and select one that fits your situation. Otherwise, you may find that the standard plan is unsuitable. After all, it is called the "default" plan.

## Know your options

For most student loans, you'll have six months from the time you leave school before you have to start student loan repayment. You can use this time to get financially settled and to weigh your repayment options.

Certain online resources are critical. Federal Student Aid's website – **studentaid.gov** – should be your first stop for repayment resources like videos, infographics, and helpful publications. Student Aid will outline several repayment plan options and help explain which one is best suited to your needs.

### What if I don't know my loans?

Okay, so you recall signing a lot of loan documents in your college years; but, you did not keep an accurate record of what you borrowed. No worries. The National Student Loan Database (http://nslds.ed.gov) can show you all of the Federal loans you have. You will need your Federal Student Aid ID to log in.

For private loans, review your credit report if you have any doubt what loans you have. Remember, you are entitled to one free copy of your credit reports every 12 months from each of the three main credit bureaus: Equifax, Experian, and TransUnion. See "Viewing your credit reports" in the chapter, "Giving You Credit."

### Stay in communication

Even if you are unemployed or experiencing any other form of financial hardship, the first rule of student loans is **stay in communication** with your loan servicer. Loan servicers will work with you to find a reasonable solution to your financial challenges.

For the sake of your credit score, you must avoid default. If you simply stop paying and stop communicating, you will unnecessarily harm your financial reputation. If you communicate, most loan servicers will work with you.

### Automate and save

Many lenders will reduce your interest rate by a quarter point or more if you automate your payments. Make sure to review this option if you are confident you can fund online payments from your bank account each month without interruption.

## Refinancing

Think twice before refinancing loans from the federal government. Make sure you are willing to forfeit loan forgiveness and lenient repayment options.

The federal government offers two compelling loan forgiveness programs – one for public servants (anyone who works for the federal, state or local government) and one for teachers. Visit studentaid.gov to learn more.

The federal government also offers income-based repayment options. You can switch to one of these options if your student loan debt payments become too burdensome.

If you refinance, you exchange federal loans for one private loan which will not qualify for loan forgiveness or income-based repayment options.

Having said this, if you are thriving in the real world – good job, consistent income, good credit – then refinancing may enable you to lock in a lower interest rate. Refinancing also allows you to consolidate several loans into one loan with one monthly payment.

Finally, if you are deducting interest from your student loans on your tax return, make sure your new loan qualifies as a student loan to the IRS. Otherwise, the interest from that loan will not be tax deductible.

## Paying more than the minimum

Paying down student loan debt is a terrific financial goal. However, this decision should happen in a larger context. Student loan holders who can pay more than the minimum each month should look at all of their debt from all sources and first pay down the debt subject to the highest interest rate.

For example, if you carry a credit card balance subject to 18% interest, and have a car loan at 6%, and a student loan with an 8% interest rate, then pay down the credit card balance while making minimum payments on the car loan and student loan.

An alternate strategy for paying down debt is offered by Dave Ramsey, the debt-busting guru. He swears by the "snowball method." In the snowball method, you first pay off your smallest loan. Ramsey claims that completely eliminating a loan feels so good that it motivates the borrower to pay down more debt.

## Prioritizing surplus cash

If you are considering paying more than the minimum due on your student loans, then make this decision in the context of worthy alternatives. Review the chapter, "The New Way to Save."

### Interest rates

We all know that lenders make money by charging customers interest when they borrow money. What is less well known is the typical amount charged on various loans.

Smart people make it their business to know how to distinguish a good interest rate from an inflated one. They visit sites like bankrate.com to learn what folks with the best credit are charged for car loans, mortgages, personal loans and credit cards.

### Best rates as of July 2022

30-year fixed mortgage: 5.3%
48-month car loan:  4.71%
Personal loan: 5.95%
Credit card:  16.74%

Source:  BankRate.com

Perhaps you have considered getting a car loan. Compare the rate you would pay to the rate offered to customers with the best credit. If yours is worse, then you will pay more to borrow money to buy a car.

For example, if the best 48-month rate you can get is 7% while the best customers pay 4.71%, then you will pay $754 more in interest over the life of the 48-month loan.

You may also wonder why the interest charged on car or home loans is significantly less than interest on a credit card balance. One reason is that car loans and mortgages are secured loans. There is an underlying asset (the car or home) that can be sold to repay the loan in case of default.

Credit card loans are unsecured. There is no asset a lender can seize if you don't pay your credit card bills.

## Paying too much

If you are a typical twentysomething, you are bombarded with credit card offers and may even get e-mails about personal loans. Perhaps you think easy access to loans has always been the norm.

In the past, loans were much more difficult to obtain. People had to prove their creditworthiness or they were denied the chance to borrow.

It is the opinion of this author that **twentysomethings face an incredibly dangerous new reality. Instead of being denied loans, they are granted loans with absurdly high interest rates.**

You owe it to yourself to compare interest rates. Walk away from any loan that carries a substantially higher interest rate than the rate the best customers get charged.

## Car Loans

Most financial planners agree that leasing a car is almost always a bad deal. Borrowing to buy a car is fine under two conditions. Only accept a loan that carries a competitive interest rate and avoid loans that take longer than 60 months to repay.

Remember that lending standards have changed. Just because you can get the loan does not mean you should take it.

To find out if you can afford all the costs associated with a car, make sure to read Chapter 4, "The Process℠: Six Steps for Living within Your Means."

## Credit Cards

If you are serious about managing money well, then you must pay off your credit card bills in full every month. Seriously, the zombies in *The Walking Dead* are smarter than you if you pay upwards of 17% interest on anything.

CHAPTER 8

# The New Way to Save

Few twentysomethings fully understand savings options that lower their tax bill. They are also unclear which to do first – save or pay down debt. Some even turn to cryptocurrency to stash cash when they would be much better served putting money elsewhere.

The list on the next page helps twentysomethings prioritize saving and debt reduction. It ranks options based on their potential for lowering taxes, saving on interest rate charges, and making money.

See next page.

### Prioritizing Surplus Cash
Contribute to 401(k) if employer offers a match
Pay off credit card debt
Contribute to a 401(k), Roth 401(k) or Roth IRA
Build an emergency fund
Invest in yourself (networking, training, dressing for success)
Pay down debt – highest interest rate first
Insurance check-up
Regular saving

### What the heck is a 401(k)?
In much the same way your parents have never heard of TikToks while you are obsessed with them, older adults love tax-advantaged retirement accounts while younger people are unfamiliar with them.

The 401(k) is named after the subsection of the U.S. Tax Code that essentially created it. According to the Investment Company Institute, 401(k)s "allow workers to contribute a portion of their pay into a tax-advantaged investment account. Participants defer taxes on their contributions until those funds are taken out of the account in retirement."

In other words, wages diverted to a 401(k) do not count as income on your federal tax return. Investment gains inside a 401(k) are not taxed until you start to withdraw money from it. 401(k)s are offered through employers. If your employer does not offer a 401(k), then see the section "IRAs."

### Roth 401(k)

What's better than lowering your tax bill now? For some, the lure of no tax on withdrawals is more exciting than tax savings today. Roth 401(k)s are funded with after-tax dollars. With a Roth, you skip the immediate tax break offered through a regular 401(k). However, you pay no tax when you finally access the money after age 59 ½.

### IRAs

IRAs are Individual Retirement Accounts. If you don't have access to a 401(k) through work, then you can enjoy similar tax advantages through an IRA.

If you just tuned out because it sounds too hard to open an IRA, then tune back in. Reach out to Vanguard (www.vanguard.com) or T.Rowe Price (www.troweprice). Both are low cost investment firms that will hold your hand through the process.

You also have the option to fund a Roth IRA. Like the Roth 401(k), Roth IRAs are funded with after-tax dollars. Instead of an immediate tax break, Roth IRAs offer no tax on withdrawals as long as you wait until age 59 ½ to access your money.

### 401(k) match

If your employer matches your 401(k) contributions, then saving in your 401(k) is your number one priority. The match and the tax breaks put your savings on steroids.

### Pay off credit card debt

If your employer does not match your 401(k) contributions, then paying off credit cards is your #1 priority. Borrowing money at a rate of 18 - 25% is ludicrous.

### Do I have to pay down credit card debt first?

No. Reasonable people will argue that 401(k) contributions are better than credit card debt reduction for three reasons: automatic savings, tax savings, and gains from investments in your 401(k).

If you are in the 12% federal tax bracket and the investments inside your 401(k) do well, then funding your 401(k) can be equal to or better than paying down credit card debt. However, if the underlying investments lose value (think stock market declines), then paying down credit card debt is better.

This author loathes credit card debt. Your mom, best friend, and uncle are welcome to disagree.

### Build an emergency fund

An emergency fund allows you to manage mishaps like job loss without incurring credit card debt. The amount you should save depends on how easily you can replace your job in case of job loss. Set aside at least $1,000 for emergencies.

## Invest in yourself

If you can increase your income through networking, training or dressing for success, then it's time to invest in you.

Could you potentially earn more if you were a better public speaker? Does your appearance make a good impression? Is there someone you can take out to lunch who could recommend you for a job that pays more?

Spending spare cash on networking, training, and dressing for success is investing in yourself. You may be surprised by the returns.

## Pay down loans

As mentioned in the chapter, "Student Loans and Other Debt," paying down debt is a terrific financial goal. However, make sure you know which loans to eliminate first. Look at all of your debt from all sources and first pay down the debt subject to the highest interest rate.

For example, if you carry a credit card balance subject to 18% interest, and have a car loan at 6%, and a student loan with an 8% interest rate, then pay down the credit card balance while making minimum payments on the car loan and student loan.

An alternate strategy for paying down debt is offered by Dave Ramsey, the debt-busting guru. He swears by the "snowball method." In the snowball method, you first pay off your smallest loan. Ramsey claims that completely eliminating a loan feels so good that it motivates the borrower to pay down more debt.

### Insurance check-up

If lack of money was an obstacle to purchasing insurance coverage, then make sure to review your insurance needs now that you have more cash. For example, renters insurance is relatively inexpensive and protects you against theft, fire, and other random bad luck like a pipe bursting in the apartment above yours. Check out the next chapter, "Risk Management," to make sure you are covered.

### Regular savings

Finally! Now you can save outside of a retirement account for short term goals. When you save, limit risky investments (hello, cryptocurrency) to 10% of all savings.

### Mix it up

If you are taking steps to eliminate credit card debt, then you can put your surplus cash in two or more of the options listed, simultaneously.

For example, you can contribute $50 per paycheck into your 401(k), and pay down credit card balances, and get renters insurance.

Good luck with your debt-busting and saving!

CHAPTER 9

# Risk Management

In the hilarious movie *Pitch Perfect*, acapella singers are dismissed from their new singing group for violating a ridiculous, drunken oath ("I solemnly promise to never have sexual relations with a Treblemaker or may my vocal chords be ripped out by wolves"). When the lead character, Beca (Anna Kendrick), is shocked by the swift dismissals, she exclaims, "That oath was serious?!" The domineering leader of the singing group replies, "Dixie Chick serious."

Like it or not, the adult world can be Dixie Chick serious. You may find you are as baffled as Anna Kendrick's character when swift punishment follows minor offense. For example, in some states, **landlords can begin eviction proceedings if rent is one** *week* **late**. They can also legally remove you based on the naughty behavior of your roommate (yes, you both have to go).

Dixie. Chick. Serious.

In a Dixie Chick serious world, twentysomethings need to consider these common threats to their financial well-being:

Loss of income
Spike in expenses
Legal Limbo

### Loss of income
As an employed person, you generate a consistent stream of income. That's why financial planners want you to think of yourself as an asset in need of protection.

While insurance products are used to minimize risk, start with common sense. Protect your ability to work by protecting yourself. Wear the helmet. Check for ticks. Don't leave the bar at midnight to walk home alone. And that hobby that requires a skill saw? Maybe not.

Staying healthy to meet the demands of your job is your first priority. The second? Protect your job by developing a service mentality.

Bosses love employees who get the needs of the organization and proactively meet them. Energetic, service-minded employees have more job security than their competent but self-absorbed peers.

Be especially careful with bosses who act like friends. Don't let their mixed signals confuse you. Bosses are not like parents, teachers, and coaches who had your best interest at heart. Bosses want what is best for the organization.


## Emergency fund
An emergency fund is a form of self-insurance. If you lose your job or can't work, then an emergency fund allows you to cover current expenses without incurring credit card debt.

How much to save in an emergency fund depends on your monthly expenses and how easily you can get a new job if you lose your current one. An emergency fund is not meant to cover a long stretch of unemployment due to an accident or illness. That's the goal of disability insurance.


## Disability insurance
Sometimes, you can take every precaution and still get slammed by bad luck. What would happen if you had a bad accident or a major illness?

If you are a twentysomething, then you probably grew up watching AFLAC commercials. The commercials featured a duck who said "Aflac" instead of "quack." The tagline was, "If you are hurt and miss work, it won't hurt to miss work." This is the premise of disability coverage. It's a form of insurance where you pay a set amount to guarantee a future income if you can't work.

According to the Insurance Information Institute, many employers offer some form of disability insurance. However, you need to reach out to your HR department to find out how to get covered.

### Speaking of insurance

Before you look into insurance, be prepared to see familiar words like "policy" and "premium" used in ways you don't recognize.

In his book, *How to Speak Money,* John Lanchester argues that the language of money is difficult because key terms don't mean what they do in everyday life. For example, in the world of money, "security" is a noun and means "any financial instrument that can be traded like an asset."

As you start to learn new money terms like "hedge fund" (which doesn't hedge anything), do not try to infer meaning. Simply google the term and add its money context. For example, to understand the term, "premium," as it relates to insurance, google "insurance premium."

To help you get started, below are the key insurance terms you need to know when you shop for insurance.

**Premium** – what you pay for insurance coverage

**Policy** – the insurance contract that outlines what is covered, the premium, and other important factors like your deductible.

**Deductible** – the amount you pay before your insurance starts to cover the costs outlined in your claim.

**Claim** – the request you make to the insurance company to cover an expense.

## Spike in expenses

Research shows that twentysomethings are optimistic about the future. That's great. An upbeat attitude will give you energy and resilience. However, optimism can backfire if you have no money set aside for the unexpected.

If your finances only work if nothing goes wrong, then your finances don't work; something always goes wrong.

Your car will get towed because you didn't see the no parking sign. Your sketchy roommate will move out without giving ample notice. Your hours at work will get reduced.

Having an **emergency fund** is the best way to make sure you don't wrack up credit card debt in an imperfect world.

### Renters Insurance

Imagine you had to replace your clothes, new mattress, expensive bedding, and more because of a fire that started in the apartment below yours. How could you handle this spike in expenses? If you had renters insurance, then you'd be fine.

Renters insurance is relatively inexpensive and covers a range of risks like theft, fire, and water damage. Most large insurance companies have user-friendly websites that make getting a renters insurance quote very easy.

In fact, visiting a few sites and getting quotes is a smart way to get used to the idea of purchasing insurance. You may be surprised how simple and inexpensive it is to get good coverage.

### Health Insurance

Unexpected medical bills can devastate your finances. Health insurance is a MUST.

Typically, a young adult can stay on a parent's health insurance plan until age 26. Alternately, you may have access to health coverage through work.

If you cannot get health coverage through a parent's plan or work, then visit Healthcare.gov to find your best option. Healthcare.gov is run by the federal government and helps people shop for and enroll in affordable health insurance.

## Life Insurance

In the past, young adults with no children were told they did not need life insurance. Today, that decision is more complicated.

Even if no one is depending on you, your parents may have taken out loans to put you through college. Those loans must be repaid even in the event of your untimely death.

If you are young and healthy, then **term life insurance** is worth a look. In most cases, term insurance is very inexpensive (believe those radio ads that say "$18 per month for $250,000 in coverage"). Why not spend a little to cover the risk of your parents' double devastation (losing you but keeping the debt)?

## Legal limbo

Most young adults can rely on a parent to help in case of an emergency. But did you know that mom or dad does not automatically have a *legal* right to handle your affairs if you get sick or injured?

Alessandra Messineo Long, an attorney in Greenwich, CT, advises her clients with adult children to execute these three documents to make sure that financial and healthcare decisions remain in the control of the family.

Durable Power of Attorney
Living Will
Healthcare Proxy

"You don't want a crisis situation to arise without these documents in place," states Messineo Long.

Legal limbo is also a threat if you don't have a Will. However, this document is usually not necessary for young, single people with no children.

As Paul Sullivan points out in his *New York Times* article, *Prince Needed a Will, But Maybe You Don't*, "most people who are not wealthy have more of their money in assets that pass to heirs through beneficiary designation forms, not Wills. These include retirement accounts, 401(k) plans and life insurance."

If you are married and/or have a child, then you do need a Will. Consult an attorney.

Glad we had this talk.

CHAPTER 10

# Managing Success

Until now, this book covered the basics. To manage money well, all twentysomethings should understand the impact of taxes on gross income; learn **The Process**℠ to eliminate overspending, and be mindful of other priorities like having health insurance and building good credit.

Beyond these fundamentals, money advice starts to depend on each person's unique situation. Take healthcare coverage. People with very low income need advice on how to apply for Medicaid. Meanwhile, people with very high income should learn the tax benefits of a Health Savings Account.

While this book could easily double in size if it considered all the possible financial circumstances of twentysomethings (like military service or single parenting), it is fitting to end on an aspirational note.

This final chapter is about managing success. It focuses on the unique challenges and opportunities faced by high earners. It also lauds twentysomethings who manage to save thousands of dollars on an average income.

### Prerequisite: Taxes 101
The chapter, "Taxes 101," is a prerequisite for financial success in general and for this chapter, in particular. Make sure you understood the main points of that chapter, especially the progressive nature of our tax system.

### Success from high income
If you took mom's advice and went into one of the STEM fields, then you may be earning $75,000 or more shortly after graduation. Due to the progressive nature of our tax code, you and other high-income twentysomethings need targeted advice to lower your taxable income.

### Magic number revisited
Your "magic number" is the point where your income crosses over into the 22% federal tax bracket. Once you hit your magic

number, taxes can take an enormous bite.

For example, here is what happens to a dollar earned in the 22% federal tax bracket if you live in New York City.

| | |
|---|---|
| $1.00 | Income |
| -0.22 | Federal tax – 22% |
| -0.08 | FICA (6.2% Social Security and 1.45% Medicare) |
| -0.06 | New York state tax – 6% |
| <u>-0.04</u> | NYC local tax – 4% |
| $ -.40 | Total |

Once New Yorkers hit the 22% federal tax bracket, they lose 40% of each dollar earned from work to taxes.

## Calculating your magic number

Your magic number will depend on your tax status. Recall from the chapter "Taxes 101" that standard deductions and tax brackets depend on filing status.

For example, in 2022, the magic number for a person filing "single" is:

| | |
|---|---|
| $12,950 | standard deduction on 2022 tax returns |
| <u>$41,775</u> | upper limit of 12% bracket |
| | |
| $54,725 | Magic number |

To calculate your magic number, select your tax status and then review the standard deduction and tax brackets for that status. Add together your standard deduction and the upper limit of the 12% bracket to get your magic number.

### Credits and deductions

Credits and deductions add a layer of complexity to the magic number concept. For example, if you have significant student loan debt and meet the requirements for deducting student loan interest, then you can make an "adjustment to income" on Schedule 1 of your 1040. While your magic number remains the same, the student loan deduction enables you to lower your taxable income. This is an added buffer before you reach your magic number.

### Exceeding your magic number

If you are in the enviable position of having income above your magic number, then you need to learn legal ways to pay less tax.

### Fund your 401(k)

If you will exceed your magic number, then you should fund your 401(k) with dollars that would otherwise be subject to the 22% federal tax. If your employer offers a match, then you should fund your 401(k) up to the match regardless of your marginal tax rate.

In 2022, you can divert up to $20,500 in wages into a 401(k). FICA taxes (Social Security and Medicare) are not reduced by 401(k) contributions. However, in most cases, you will also save on state and local taxes.

## IRAs

Regular (not Roth) IRAs mimic the tax advantages of 401(k)s. If you do not have access to a 401(k), then fund an IRA.

In 2022, IRA contributions are limited to $6,000 for adults under age 50.

## Flexible spending account

A Flexible Spending Account (FSA) allows you to pay for certain out-of-pocket health care costs using pre-tax dollars. This means you'll save an amount equal to the taxes you would have paid on the money you set aside.

If you have a health plan through a job, you can use an FSA to pay for copayments, deductibles, some drugs, and some other health care costs.

## Other tax savings

Once you are solidly in the 22% federal tax bracket, it pays to get good tax advice. You should seriously consider hiring a tax professional.

### Hiring a tax professional

Here's how to avoid scammers and find a true tax professional.

Any reputable tax preparer will have a Preparer Tax Identification Number (PTIN). This number is required by the IRS. Do not hire anyone who lacks this basic credential.

Avoid tax preparers who claim they can get you a large refund. Do not use tax preparers who base their fee on the size of the refund.

As your tax situation gets more complicated, you will want someone who can represent you before the IRS. Ask co-workers, friends, and family if they know a reputable Enrolled Agent. They are less expensive than tax attorneys and can speak to the IRS on your behalf.

Certified Public Accountants can also represent you before the IRS. They are typically more expensive than Enrolled Agents.

### Success with an average income

Some young people deserve to be called "successful" simply because they save a significant portion of their take home pay. How? Here is one telling statistic. According to bankrate.com's "cost of living calculator," an individual living in Amarillo, TX needs only $33,411 per year to enjoy the same lifestyle of a New Yorker earning $50,000.

While research is lacking, anecdotal evidence suggests that some young adults thoroughly investigate the cost of living in certain areas and intentionally move to low cost locations. If these same twentysomethings embrace frugality and avoided student loan debt, then they can save thousands each year.

If you are saving a lot on an average salary, then you might assume the advice in the beginning of this chapter is for you. Think again. Your tax liability is quite different from the tax liability of a high earner.

If you have thousands to save and your marginal tax rate is below 22%, then you are the poster child for the Roth IRA.

## Roth IRA
Every time I visit my in-laws in Maine, they point out a beautiful stretch of coastland and tell the same story. During the Great Depression, the entire parcel was for sale for only $500.00. Once the requisite gasps are done (the land is worth more than a million dollars today), the story always ends with the same line: "But no one had $500.00 in The Depression."

A similar story exists today with Roth IRAs. The ability to invest for decades and then withdraw the initial investment and all gains tax free is an extraordinary opportunity. However, who can afford to save money without an immediate tax break (remember, Roths are funded with after-tax dollars)?

If your marginal tax rate is below 22%, you don't need the immediate tax savings of a 401(k) or regular IRA. Choose the Roth.

You will thank me later.

# Epilogue

The early years of money management are like your first few years driving: you can get where you need to go without doing anything complicated like changing a tire or switching car insurance. However, it is a good idea to be somewhat prepared for greater responsibilities.

Now that you know money basics, build on your knowledge in small, consistent ways. Google money terms you don't recognize. Sign up for IRS e-mails. Have a personal finance book on your night table.

Speaking of personal finance books, the sequel to this one is in the works. Meanwhile, you can learn a great deal from these personal finance writers: Jean Chatzky, Beth Kobliner, Dave Ramsey, and Liz Weston.

If you want to laugh and learn, then check out the money section of Kelly Williams Brown's book *Adulting*. It is both hilarious and helpful.

The sequel to this book arrives Fall 2022. Until then, best of luck on your money journey.

# Notes

# Notes

## About the Author

Kristen Jacks is a financial educator and the Founder of Money in Your Twenties℠. Kristen studied financial planning at Boston University's Center for Professional Education. She started her career at *Kiplinger's Personal Finance Magazine* and later worked at *Mutual Funds Magazine*. Kristen is a graduate of Duke University.

Made in the USA
Las Vegas, NV
02 November 2022